Snake Chinese Horoscope 2024

By

IChingHun FengShuisu

Table of Contents

Introduce

The character of people born in the year of the SNAKE

People born in this year speak less and have cute faces. Anyone who sees it is likely to be persistent and charming. Loved by others, speaks little, avoids gossip, and has good manners. People this year have never been in debt, and know how to save, but are sluggish. But being a thinker is beneficial. A wise and determined individual who does not abandon anything in the middle of the road. People born in the Year of the Snake trust first impressions, feelings, sympathy, advice, and other people's opinions. incorporating the sixth sense into decision-making.

Even if he is a person who likes to talk less, when he has spoken, he often speaks exaggeratedly. Another is a good lie. No matter how big or small and survive every time. People born this year love to flirt and have sex, but not too nasty. So people come to fall in love with this year's man with a big head because they are romantic, very jealous, likes to have high expectations, wants to feel confident, and is always safe.

Strength:
You are a scholar who is intelligent and enjoys learning.

Weaknesses:
You're narcissistic and self-sufficient.

Love:
People born in this year have a lot of boyfriends. Because so much love must confront the chaos of love until it hurts. There is always a love that is so hot and flirtatious that it cannot keep up. Some people may not have a unique partnership with whom to demonstrate their charm. Old women and widows are buzzing, even though they are not attractive or attractive. because your grace's style and eloquence It's so catchy, don't tell anyone Flirting extends to even the smallest snake people. However, if someone is already a fan, I can assure you that I am the most envious. Do

not allow anyone to interfere. Most importantly, enjoy being selfish and impatient.

Suitable Career:

Because Snakes are fire-elemental, those born in the year of the Snake should pursue a career related to fire, such as opening a shop for electrical or electronic devices such as radios, and televisions, or selling electrical appliances. Open a gas station, or pursue a career that necessitates specific skills, such as being a speaker, critic, judge, prosecutor, teacher, writer, politician, journalist, beautician, photographer, makeup artist, or model. Modeling, selling artificial plants, trees, and flowers, fortune telling in various fields, the military, and law enforcement are all suitable professions for those born in the year of the Snake.

Year of the SNAKE (Gold) | (1941) & (2001)

"The Snake in hibernation" is a person born in the year of the SNAKE at the age of 83 years (1941) and 23 years (2001)

Overview

This year is considered an excellent period for teens because favorable stars come into the house of destiny, generating a force of assistance and support. Make academic or professional advancement. It's time to relax. As a result, diligence and learning diligence are crucial components in pioneering and building. You must have the determination to fight hard this year. Gain experience by creating things that look patient. Efforts and outcomes will not be overlooked. Adults will view skill as a potential for advancement and a bright future. But because during the year, an evil star called "Huay Yim" circles and harasses. Which will readily expand its impact, resulting in mishaps while working and utilizing various tools and equipment. Traveling is included in the usage of the road. As a result, you must be more cautious. Because it poses a risk of injury and hemorrhage. Also, when meeting with friends this year, be wary of getting caught up in squabbles. If you control your impatience. It will help you improve your security.

This life cycle is for seniors in the Year of the Snake since the planets that circle into your home of destiny this year are Tek Satellites, resulting in a profitable career or business. There is nothing to be concerned about. However, during the year, you must be wary of the wicked stars who extend their power and influence as well. Cause health issues and accident hazards. As a result, items that must be prioritized this year are unavoidable. When it comes to health care, avoid getting too engaged or intervening in your children's issues. It will make everyone pleased.

Career and Business

Work for those destined for the Year of the Snake, since this year has the power of patronage from the fortunate star Tiang Tek to encourage it. Please embark on a challenging task. Please be persistent and bold in your pursuit. The power of this year's success is pretty positive. You will discover growth and prosperity whether you are working or conducting business. Starting a new career, investing in equities, and investing through multiple avenues. This year is looking promising. You may invest in whatever you have a personal interest in, as long as you have a strategy and cash available. Throughout the month, that work business comprises several investments. You will find progress and prosperity including the 12th Chinese month (6 Jan. - 3 Feb.), the 2nd Chinese month (5 Mar. - 3 Apr.), the 4th Chinese month (5 May - 4 Jun.), and the 8th Chinese month (7 Sep. – 7 Oct.)

As for the months where work will be disrupted and obstacles will arise, they are the 1st Chinese month (4 Feb. - 4 Mar.), the 5th Chinese month (5 Jun. - 5 Jul.), the 7th Chinese month (7 Aug. – 6 Sep.) and the 10th Chinese month (7 Nov. – 5 Dec.). Be wary of mistakes made by juniors or coworkers. If you have to sign any contracts this year, you must be more discreet. Be wary of contract details that might lead to problems in the future.

Financial

The financial fortunes of this year are mediocre. Salary or sales income meets the required conditions. Money expected from gambling or a windfall, on the other hand, might be considered to be acquired or lost. Particularly during the months of the 1st Chinese month (4 Feb. - 4 Mar.), the 5th Chinese month (5 Jun. - 5 Jul.), the 7th Chinese month (7 Aug.- 6 Sep.) and the 10th Chinese month (7 Nov. - 5 Dec.). It is recommended to avoid gambling. Make no loans to anyone or sign any promises. This is because there have been incidences of mischief and harassment at the House of Destiny this year. As a result, you are severely forbidden from dealing in pirated goods and criminal activities. As for the months in which your finances are flowing smoothly, they are the 12th Chinese month (6 Jan. - 3 Feb.), the 2nd Chinese month (5 Mar. - 3 Apr.), the 4th Chinese month (5 May. – 4 Jun.) and the 8th Chinese month (7 Sep. – 7 Oct.).

Family

This year's horoscope revealed a combination of positive and bad things for the family. You must pay greater attention to the safety of the members of the home due to the influence of the bad star Huay Yim, which sends power to disturb and upset you. Because you may get injured and bleed out. You should also look after the health of the individuals in your home. Especially during the 1st Chinese month (4 Feb. - 4 Mar.), the 5th Chinese month (5 Jun. - 5 Jul.), the 7th Chinese month (7 Aug.- 6 Sep.), and the 10th Chinese month (7 Nov. - 5 Dec.), the health of youngsters and the elderly at home must be properly checked. In addition, you must be careful of valuables being damaged, lost, or stolen.

Love

This year is nice and attractive for young Destiny's love. The opposite sex will be fascinated. Some people may find their soul mate and have an ideal moment to be married or get married this year. Even if love and relationships are wonderful, you should be cautious during the following months, when your love is relatively weak and disagreements are common, namely: 1st Chinese month (4 Feb. - 4 Mar.), 5th Chinese month (5 Jun. - 5 Jul.), 7th Chinese month (7 Aug. - 6 Sep.), and 10th Chinese month (7 Nov. - 5 Dec.). Be cautious of arguments. Be wary of extraneous persons interfering and separating you from your relationship.

Health

This year, the destined person's health meets the standards in both age cycles and must be closely observed. Because the bad star Huay Yim collides with the base of the health horoscope, its influence will spread into focus. As a result, you must use caution. Health issues should be avoided by elders. Especially fatty acids that block the arteries, coronary artery disease, high blood pressure, heart disease, and slips and falls that cause damage and bleeding. Young people should be cautious of accidents both at work and on the road, and there may be risks associated with mourning for older family or sick senior relatives who may exhibit more severe symptoms. During the months when the destined person in both life cycles has to pay additional care and attention to their health, specifically the 1st Chinese month (4 Feb. - 4 Mar.), and the 5th Chinese month (5 Jun. - 5 Jul.), 7th Chinese month (7 Aug. - 6 Sep.) and 10th Chinese month (7 Nov. - 5 Dec.) Seniors should make frequent appointments with their doctors. If you see any changes in your body, you should consult a doctor right away. This is done to keep frostbite from spreading.

Year of the SNAKE (Water) | (1953) & (2013)

" The SNAKE in the grass " is a person born in the year of the SNAKE at the age of 71 years (1953) and 11 years (2013)

Overview

The age cycle of the senior destined person of the Year of the Snake is 71 years. Even if the chosen house looks to have a set of hostile stars centered on it this year. As a result, work will be hampered. There may be job transfers or big changes at work, and disagreements between workers may occur, generating problems. However, it is considered fortunate because throughout the year, the auspicious star "Tiang Tek" circles in to show brightly and provide assistance. As a result, it can assist in mitigating some of the tragedy. But, no matter what, you should use extreme caution; it will be safer. You must be particularly cautious this year if your job requires the use of tools or equipment. Because you might get injured and bleed. Avoid stumbling and falling when walking on high or low surfaces. High blood pressure, heart disease, blood disorders, and diabetes should all be avoided. Furthermore, if you notice anything strange in your body, such as a lump or soreness in a specific region. You should consult a doctor right away for a checkup and treatment. Diseases that are begun have a greater chance of being healed than diseases that are left to continue. They are tough to treat and should be approached with caution. You should know how to let go and not worry about your children or grandkids, since this might harm your physical health.

Because the planets that are orbiting into the child's destiny house this year are This year's "Satellite" will have the ability to market itself through like. As a consequence, children will be adored by everyone in the house as well as others who see them. There will be advancements in learning. As a result, the intended individual should focus on studies this year. Review what you've learned regularly to ensure that you thoroughly comprehend it. If you have any questions, please contact the teacher. It will assist in reaching the necessary levels of academic success. However, there are certain things to be aware of: travel accidents and outdoor activities. You should be especially cautious of the danger of injury and bleeding from sharp items, hitting hard objects, or losing your balance and falling. As a result, don't forget a little precautionary safety because unforeseen events may occur.

Career and Business

This year, your senior's work or business is in good shape. As a result, you should seek a successor or helper to help you continue the job and studies and take care of fresh assets that are predicted to yield the desired profits. This year will see improvement in the education of the chosen kid. You will be able to advance and achieve better grades if you intend to work more and more diligently. Teachers and parents will like both. The months in which both work and education have outstanding progress include the 12th Chinese month (6 Jan. - 3 Feb.), the 2nd Chinese month (5 Mar. - 3 Apr.), the 4th Chinese month (5 May - 4 Jun), and 8th Chinese month (7 Sep - 7 Oct.). For the months where your work and trade will be disrupted and have problems, include the

Chinese 1st month. (4 Feb. – 4 Mar.) 5th Chinese month (5 Jun. – 5 Jul.), 7th Chinese month (7 Aug. – 6 Sep.), and 10th Chinese month (7 Nov. - 5 Dec.) Conflicts inside organizations or divisions should be avoided. Be wary of disagreements with clients, business partners, or other individuals with whom you must interact. You should also be wary of contracts that include hidden terms that might be exploited. Furthermore, in terms of establishing joint venture stocks and other investments. You should refrain during the unfriendly month. Because insiders will bring damage and corruption.

Financial

Financially, this year is not going well, and there is a possibility of losing assets. As a result, one should not be greedy or greedy. If you are greedy for money, you may have to give it to yourself. very during the months when financial leaks are very high, such as the 1st Chinese month (4 Feb. - 4 Mar.), the 5th Chinese month (5 Jun. - 5 Jul.), the 7th Chinese month (7 Aug. - 6 Sep.), and the 10th month of China (7 Nov. - 5 Dec.). Do not lend money to others or sign financial commitments. Do not bet or gamble. Do not invest in unlawful firms as this may result in a lawsuit. Also, don't be duped by enticing statements.

Family

Sharp Blood Stars and Chain Stars are bothering the House of Destiny this year. As a result, people in the home suffer from health issues. Unexpected circumstances may occur, and members of the household may have conflicts that produce disagreements. Additionally, significant assets must be closed. Don't wear it to attract thieves. Because they may be assaulted and robbed. As a result, you should be extra cautious, especially during the 1st Chinese month (4 Feb - 4 Mar), the 5th Chinese month (5 Jun - 5 Jul), the 7th Chinese month (7 Aug. - 6 Sep.), and the 10th Chinese month (7 Nov. - 5 Dec.). Avoid arguing in the house and arguing with neighbors.

Love

The love and relationship horoscope for this year is favorable. Seniors will be loved and cared for by everyone around them. They will also be able to take their wives on excursions. Participate in meritorious activities or go to see distant relatives both domestically and internationally. It is seen as a recompense for a life that has seen heat and cold up to the present day, as well as if you faithfully pay reverence to the Buddha and build merit. Life will be tranquil and pleasant in the end. Even if some love and care for the kids of this year, you must be humble. Being playful like a youngster may sometimes lead to disaster. However, seniors should be careful during the months when love is fragile and some conflicts will occur, including the 1st Chinese month (4 Feb.- 4 Mar.), the 5th Chinese month (5 Jun. - 5 Jul.), the 7th Chinese month (7 Aug. - 6 Sep.) and 10th Chinese month (7 Nov. - 5 Dec.).

Health

This year is not a favorable criterion since the home is afflicted by both malefic stars Huay Yim and Kuang Sao. This will have an impact on a variety of health issues, including blood illnesses, high blood pressure, heart disease, liver disease, diabetes, food poisoning, and other infectious diseases. As a result, you must practice good drinking and eating habits. Particularly during the 1st Chinese month (4 Feb.- 4 Mar.), the 5th Chinese month (5 Jun. - 5 Jul.), the 7th Chinese month (7 Aug.- 6 Sep.), and the 10th Chinese month (7 Nov. - 5 Dec.). In addition to keeping an eye out for irregularities in the body, elders should see a doctor on time. To obtain blood for illness analysis. You must also be cautious of possible hazards. Use electrical tools and equipment with caution. Be more cautious when traveling and utilizing the road. To keep youngsters safe from harm and bleeding. Be cautious of mishaps if you must drive large distances or visit unfamiliar areas during this period.

Year of the SNAKE (Wood) | (1965)

" The snake of merit" is a person born in the year of the SNAKE at the age of 59 years (1965)

Overview

Around this age, the auspicious stars "Thian Tek" and the stars Hok Chae moved in to assist and encourage the chosen person's residence. This is another good year in which we will be blessed with prosperity and fortune. Wealth, fame, prestige, and power will follow. It will also result in work progress. Business will thrive. Many events will go as planned. Furthermore, fortunate power visits the family riches. As a consequence, this year there will be an opportunity to host an auspicious event or a large birthday celebration (Tua Sayik) so that children and grandchildren may join in celebrating and considering meeting relatives. There is an excellent moment to move into a new house, or the house may welcome more new members. It is regarded as auspicious during auspicious times. In terms of employment, it is appropriate to identify an heir to assist in continuing the task and can be released to take care of new investments. To broaden the company's base to expand further. However, due to the arrival of negative constellations during the year, notably the "Bua Sing Star" and "Kuang Sao Star," it is another year when job or business in the month is not supportive, and you should consider it.

Be cautious before proceeding. Planning or carrying out any task. You should consider preparation in all aspects. In terms of money, be wary of minor theft or embezzlement, which can result in asset loss and issues with working capital liquidity. It also leads to health problems or diseases as a result of cumulative stress. It has an overpowering influence on the body's fire element. You must exercise caution since it can result in high blood pressure, heart disease, and blood illnesses, as well as the danger of damage and bleeding. To be safe, you should be cautious and take care of yourself and your family.

Career and Business

The work horoscope for this year is favorable. It's a larger seat. As a result, people who work full-time have the opportunity to advance in their careers. Those who do business will have the option to build additional branches, and factories, develop product lines, or invest in new and exciting enterprises.

The months in which work and business are prosperous and progressing are the 12th Chinese month (6 Jan. - 3 Feb.), the 2nd Chinese month (5 Mar. - 3 Apr.), the 4th Chinese month (5 May - 4 Jun), and the 8th Chinese month (7 Sep. - 7 Oct.), However, this is because wicked stars are orbiting the work base this year. This will expand its effect and result in a variety of issues, including internal agency disputes. There may be disagreements with consumers or business partners, as well as issues with government authorities such as the Revenue Department, and so on. You may also discover that some significant clients have relocated their orders to other locations. Especially during the months when work and business will have problems and chaos, including the 1st Chinese month (4 Feb. - 4 Mar.), the 5th Chinese month (5 Jun. - 5 Jul.), 7 Chinese months (7 Aug. – 6 Sep.) and 10th Chinese month (7 Nov. – 5 Dec.).

Financial

This year's income and finances are in terrific shape. You should enhance your pursuit and diligence. You can also utilize the funds to invest in outside firms. Will be able to extend work, create branches, and develop additional factories, allowing the company to grow to a larger scale. Especially during months when funds are flowing nicely. There is substantial income flowing in, including the 12th Chinese month (6 Jan. - 3 Feb.), the 2nd Chinese month (5 Mar. - 3 Apr.), the 4th Chinese month (5 May - 4 June), and the 8th Chinese month (7 Sept. – 7 Oct.)

As for the months when finances will be tight, there will be problems and there may be unexpected expenses that interfere, including the 1st month of China (4 Feb. - 4 Mar.), the 5th month of China (5 Jun. - 5 Jul.), 7th Chinese month (7 Aug. - 6 Sep.) and 10th Chinese month (7 Nov. - 5 Dec.).
During this time, lending, lending, or offering guarantees to close individuals should be avoided, and you should not invest in unlawful

or immoral companies. Also, be wary of thieves when leaving the house.

Family

This year's horoscope for your family will be a combination of good and negative. This is due to the presence of three evil stars in this base, including the Kuang Sao star, the Buang Sing star, and the Huai Yim star. However, if you have the opportunity to host an auspicious event in your home this year, the auspicious energy will assist in easing the auspicious energy to some level. However, the misery caused by the evil star persists. As a result, you cannot afford to be reckless about mishaps that may harm you or others in your house. Especially the threat of injury, blood, and disease.

Misfortune that results in property loss, especially during the 1st Chinese month (4 Feb. - 4 Mar.), the 5th Chinese month (5 Jun. - 5 Jul), the 7th Chinese month (7 Aug. - 6 Sep.), and the 10th Chinese month (7 Nov. - 5 Dec.), when you should be extra cautious. You should also be more cautious about having your things stolen or tricked by thieves.

Love

The love this year is mild. Although there are several points of contention. However, there is no such thing as a tipping point. Everything will be alright if you just give in. This year, your destiny will allow you to take your spouse on a sightseeing excursion. Paying tribute to the Lord Buddha, creating merit, volunteering to aid society, or commemorating a wedding anniversary will enhance and sweeten love. However, you should exercise caution during the months when disputes are likely, including the 1st Chinese month (4 Feb. - 4 Mar.), the 5th Chinese month (5 Jun. - 5 July), the 7th Chinese month (7 Aug. - 6 Sep.) and the 10th Chinese month (7 Nov. - 5 Dec.). You should not meddle with other people's families' internal connections and should avoid attending entertainment places. You must maintain control of your actions and not stray from the road. Your children and grandkids will respect, love, and honor you for a long time.

Health

This year, health issues are not going well. It's because the body has been working long and hard. It will get you as fit as you were when you were young and elderly. It is not feasible. What you can do is limit your hard activities, let go, and get adequate rest. Set aside time to exercise to help you stay young. However, you should be wary of the Fire element being overused this year. If you are agitated, the Fire element will enter your blood and heart. There may be sickness as a result. As a result, you should consume more cooling vegetables or look for herbs like Chrysanthemum juice and Luo Han Guo juice.

It will boost the chilly element while decreasing the hot element. During the 1st Chinese month (4 Feb. - 4 Mar.), the 5th Chinese month (5 June - 5 July), the 7th Chinese month (7 Aug. – 6 Sept.), and the 10th Chinese month (7 Nov. – 5 Dec.) you should pay special attention to food and eating cleanliness. Be more cautious about mishaps. If you feel your body is not up to it, if you are weak, dizzy, or have a headache, you should seek medical attention immediately.

Year of the SNAKE (Fire) | (1977)

" The SNAKE evolves from the cave" is a person born in the year of the SNAKE at the age of 47 years (1977)

Overview

This year is considered auspicious for anyone born in the Year of the Snake around this age. Auspicious stars were spotted circling to shine at the mansion of fate. Because of its patronage power, it will aid in the advancement of work and business. You must have the confidence to invest and to start your firm. Those who do business will see significant growth this year. There is a possibility to build branches, buy a firm, or buy shares to take over the company (become a majority shareholder) or to purchase other pricey assets. It is simple to organize a variety of events. The labor activities face relatively minor stumbling blocks. It also looked like the dwelling was imbued with the force of good fortune. Moving into a new house or habitation is an auspicious period for the person of fate. A favorable incident will occur at home. There is a possibility to bring in new family members. However, you must be cautious of the threats posed by the wicked stars that revolve throughout the year, notably Dao Huai Yim and Dao Kuang Sa. The existence of these malevolent constellations and their growing influence has had an effect. This frequently leads to disagreement inside the organization. A mistake was made with a consumer, business partner, or government agency. There will be difficulties and harm as a result. People in the house will bicker and quarrel with one another. You should not disregard health issues. Accidents at work and on the road, in particular. Take care not to harm yourself to the point of bleeding while using or working with equipment or machines. Another concern that should not be disregarded since the devil is a violent player is an increasing preoccupation with vices or a desire to frequent entertainment places. This necessitates the application of awareness and self-control. Allowing your thoughts to wander will lead to discontent in your life.

Career and Business

This year's work is seen to be in good form, and a prosperous route has been discovered. Work will be completed successfully. Business will thrive. It is once again a terrific moment for those of you who are considering expanding or seeking a chance to start a business, be your boss, grow, create extra branches, or engage in new ventures. Such opportunities do not come along very frequently. If you pass up this opportunity, you will never have another. Especially during the months when work and business are going well, such as the 12th Chinese month (6 Jan. - 3 Feb.), and the 2nd Chinese month (5 Mar. - 3 Apr.). The 4th Chinese month (5 May - 4 Jun.) and the 8th Chinese month (7 Sep.-7 Oct.) During this time, you may make good money by investing in new firms. However, you must be cautious because some people with malicious intentions may come in to obstruct, disrupt, and cause trouble. Especially during the months when labor will be difficult and difficult, such as the 1st Chinese month (4 Feb. - 4 Mar.), the 5th Chinese month (5 Jun - 5 Jul.), the 7th Chinese month (7 Aug. -

6 Sep.), and the 10th Chinese month (7 Nov. - 5 Dec.). Be wary about getting duped by fraudsters. Be aware that there may be nuances in negotiating or accepting employment that will place you at a disadvantage. Keep an eye out for internal tensions and disagreements with outsiders.

Financial

In terms of financial fortune, this year will be prosperous. Please be alert and conscientious. Dare to invest in business growth. Investing in new ventures These are all excellent ways to boost your account balance. The months when your finances are flowing smoothly include the 12th Chinese month (6 Jan. - 3 Feb.), the 2nd Chinese month (5 Mar. - 3 Apr.), the 4th Chinese month (5 May. - 4 Jun), and the 8th Chinese month (7 Sep. - 7 Oct.). The months when your finances are disrupted include the 1st Chinese month (4 Feb. - 4 Mar), the 5th Chinese month (5 Jun - 5 Jul), the 7th Chinese month (7 Aug. - 6 Sep.), and the 10th Chinese month (7 Nov. – 5 Dec.) During this time, you should not make any new or extra investments. Because you have the right to be duped. Do not bet or gamble. Do not lend money to others or sign financial commitments. You should not be greedy. Avoid investing in companies that are likely to break the law. In addition to losing property as a result of being fined and penalized, you may face additional criminal charges.

Family

This year will provide excellent prosperity and fortunate work. Many things went as planned. There will be an opportune moment in the house for getting engaged, getting married, and relocating. Moving to a new office, or new members may be added to the house. However, it is in the 1st Chinese month (4 Feb. - 4 Mar.), the 5th Chinese month (5 Jun. - 5 Jul.), the 7th Chinese month (7 Aug. - 6 Sep.), and the 10th Chinese month (7 Nov. - 5 Dec.). Be wary of squabbles and disagreements among household members. You should also be wary of minors in the house causing disturbance or getting into issues with neighbors. Be wary about valuables being misplaced, damaged, or stolen. Also, use caution while using machine tools or you may injure yourself. In addition to being concerned about house safety, outdated or broken installations should be fixed or replaced. Don't allow it to fall and injure anyone in the home.

Love

This year, your love horoscope is good. There was pampering, no dissatisfaction. Even though there were some conflicts or conflicts, it was not serious. Therefore, it is considered a good opportunity for you to take your beloved spouse on a trip to a distant land or to go together to make merit and pay homage to the Buddha and ask for blessings, all of which will help add sweetness to your married life. However, there are some months that you have to be careful of where conflicts and resentments can easily occur, including the 1st Chinese month (4 Feb. - 4 Mar.), the 5th Chinese month (5 Jun. - 5 Jul), 7th Chinese month (7 Aug. - 6 Sep.) and 10th Chinese month (7 Nov. - 5 Dec.) Do not get involved or be a third party in other people's families. You should avoid going to places of entertainment because it will only lead to conflicts. You may also contract the disease again.

Health

This year, your health is not in excellent shape. It might be due to your heavy workload. Excessive stress or a lack of sleep might cause existing ailments to resurface. If you split your time wisely by exercising and getting enough sleep. It will assist in improving your health. The first Chinese month (4 Feb. - 4 Mar.), the fifth Chinese month (5 Jun - 5 Jul), the seventh Chinese month (7 Aug - 6 Sep), and the tenth Chinese month (7 Nov - 5 Dec) are the months to pay special attention to your health. Furthermore, you must be more cautious on the road. To avoid harm and bleeding. When consuming food, you should practice good hygiene since infections might enter through the mouth. Take precautions against infectious illnesses, seasonal contagious diseases, air allergies, and other allergens.

Year of the SNAKE (Earth) | (1989)

"The Snake In the River" is a person born in the year of the SNAKE at the age of 35 years (1989)

Overview

This age cycle is related to the planet that orbits your house of destiny, the "Satellite Satellite," for individuals born in the Year of the Snake. This year is another good period to pay attention to. Always strive to improve yourself and use your knowledge and talents, as well as previous experiences, to help your job. This year, the condescending influence of the fortunate stars will inspire you to get promoted. Pay raise It's known as gaining both money and positions. It is thought to represent two layers of good fortune for individuals who will advance to high positions. You must be able to work effectively at upper-lower levels and coordinate relationships with various departments both inside and outside the business, in addition to having strong human relations abilities. Both require knowledge as well as talent. Morality and good behavior, learning how to honor seniors, taking care of the small ones, humility, and respect are two more things you should not omit or forget this year. As a result, it will assist to lower the risk of getting demoted. However, one must be careless or unwary of the bad luck that emanates from the terrible stars that orbit through the house of fate, notably the Buang Sing and Kuang So stars, which will affect economic troubles. At times, finances will be insufficiently liquid. You should also be concerned about the health of the elderly in the house or if unexpected occurrences occur with house members, such as health difficulties of the destined person. Attending a gathering and drinking beer must be acceptable behavior. Don't drink till you're inebriated, as this will render your body unconscious and weak. This causes the spread of other illnesses. The next stage is to avoid accidents while at work and when driving on the road. You should be cautious.

Career and Business

This year is beneficial for work since the auspicious star emerges to boost one's knowledge and talents. It will be obvious to others around you. Please demonstrate your abilities. This year, you will have the option to get promoted to a higher position, boost your pay, or start your own business. Your bosses will respect you, and your friends and subordinates will see you as a leader. It is the cornerstone for a prosperous future. Particularly during the months when your work and business are exceptional, including the 12th Chinese month (6 Jan. - 3 Feb.), the 2nd Chinese month (5 Mar. - 3 Apr.), the 4th Chinese month (5 May - 4 Jun), and the 8th Chinese month h (7 Sep - 7 Oct.). Furthermore, you will be able to enter equities or invest in businesses that will produce positive outcomes and provide sufficient dividend returns. However, you should use caution during the months when job and commercial troubles may arise, including the 1st Chinese month (4 Feb. - 4 Mar.), the 5th Chinese month (5 Jun. - 5 July), the 7th month. China (7 Aug. - 6 Sep.) and the 10th Chinese month (7 Nov. - 5 Dec.)Be cautious about being bullied. Jealous individuals are impeding development. Conflicts will inevitably emerge inside the agency. Make contracts with caution. It may conceal exploitation, which might become an issue in the future.

Financial

This year's earnings are modest. However, gambling expectations must be cautious because there is a potential of facing a crisis during the year. You will also experience property loss in situations where you did not expect to intervene. As a result, everyone who owes money should constantly inquire. Leaving the account in credit for an extended time, for example, may result in bad debt. Particularly during the 1st Chinese month (4 Feb - 4 Mar), the 5th Chinese month (5 Jun - 5 Jul), the 7th Chinese month (7 Aug - 6 Sep), and the 10th Chinese month (7 Nov - 5 Dec). Gambling is forbidden at this time. Do not lust for money that is not yours. Do not put your money into high-risk or unlawful ventures. As for the months with good financial flexibility, they are the 12th Chinese month (6 Jan. - 3 Feb.), the 2nd Chinese month (5 Mar. - 3 Apr.), the 4th Chinese month (5 May - 4 Jun) and the 8th Chinese month (7 Sep. – 7 Oct.).

Family

In terms of the family, this year will provide calm and fortunate energy. As a result, wonderful things will happen within the house. There is an option to add more members. There is a possibility to purchase pricey real estate for your house. There is an excellent time to move into a new house or property, or there will be an old birthday party. However, due to the impact of the bad stars Snao Sing and Star, which disturb the family base in the coming months, one cannot be careless. The 1st Chinese month (4 Feb - 4 Mar.), and the 5th Chinese month. (5 Jun - 5 Jul), 7th Chinese month (7 Aug - 6 Sep) and 10th Chinese month (7 Nov. - 5 Dec.) You must Take precautions to ensure the safety of the elderly in the house and keep an eye on their health. Be wary of quarrels and quarrels among family members, which might destabilize the harmony. Be wary of intruders breaking into your home.

Love

This year's love is a good criterion that masks evil. You must endeavor to maintain control and refrain from allowing the charms to fool you into attending entertainment establishments and waste your money. Don't allow your pals to lead you astray in your search for pleasure. Otherwise, there would undoubtedly be a heated debate with the real person at home. Especially during the months when love is weak and things can easily damage each other, such as the 1st Chinese month (4 Feb - 4 Mar) and the 5th Chinese month (5 Jun - 5 Jul) ,the 7th Chinese month (7 Aug - 6 Sep) and the 10th Chinese month (7 Nov. - 5 Dec) Interfere or act as a third party in other people's familial ties. Avoid going to places of entertainment.

Health

This year is not favorable for the chosen person's physical health. There will be illnesses that will bother both the body and the psyche. You should be cautious of infectious infections brought on by eating anything you want. Take care of your hygiene, including what you drink and eat. Be wary of allergies and influenza, and avoid seasonal outbreaks. You must take great care of yourself in the next months, especially: 1st Chinese month (4 Feb- 4 Mar), the 5th

Chinese month (5 Jun - 5 Jul), 7th Chinese month (7 Aug - 6 Sep), and 10th Chinese month (7 Nov- 5 Dec), be more cautious when driving and traveling. Especially following a party If you use alcohol or other intoxicants, you should not drive. To improve your health and build your immune system, you should obtain adequate rest or find time to exercise.

Chinese Astrology Horoscope for Each Month

Month 12 in the Rabbit Year (6 Jan 23 - 3 Feb 23)

The fate of people born in the Year of the Snake this month enters the alliance's domain. As a result, work continues to thrive. Commercial firms have also grown their sales and revenue. As a result, when the sky opens up this month, you should keep your dedication and resolve to work continually, and should not give up in the face of hurdles and issues. The more diligent you are, the more money you will generate that will continue to increase.

This wage puts you in a position of abundance. Your pockets will be stuffed to the brim with cash. This month will be more difficult, but it will be worthwhile. Because you work hard, the benefits are many. You will receive complete help and a prosperous route in the area of business and business. If you are trapped, rush to someone for support and assistance. As a consequence, you should rush to grow the outcomes, generate results, increase sales and money, or complete the project completely. If you don't act promptly, your excellent energy will be lost, and you can miss out on an opportunity. If you are ready, for those of you who do not yet have your own business. This month is a good opportunity to branch out and become your boss. Your manager will see your work if you are working this month. There is the possibility of being promoted or having your income increased.

There is peace inside the family, and the members love and respect one another. It's a terrific moment for single folks to find love. If you meet someone you like this month, you might be your soul mate, sharing the pillow. However, you must continue with your connection. It's not healthy for your health. Take caution not to sleep too much. The increasing fire element will lead you to cough, sneeze, get sensitive to the air, or develop other ailments, as well as make you more cautious of mishaps while traveling. Starting a new career, investing in stocks, and making other investments for family and close friends. This month, the outlook is positive, and dividends will not be reduced.

Support Days: 2 Jan., 6 Jan., 10 Jan., 14 Jan., 18 Jan., 22 Jan., 26 Jan., 30 Jan.
Lucky Days: 9 Jan., 21 Jan.
Misfortune Days: 12 Jan., 24 Jan.
Bad Days: 3 Jan., 15 Jan., 27 Jan

Month 1 in the Dragon Year (4 Feb 23 - 5 Mar 23)

As the first month of the Chinese New Year approaches, your fate has shifted to confront the opposition. There is also the arrival of lethal power from the wicked star, which is ready to disrupt and disrupt. As a result, the horoscope curve is vertically downward. During this time, you should be extremely cautious of the potential of unexpected property loss. As a result, during this month, you should approach every action with attention and tranquility. Before taking any action, take a good look around. Make careful plans for this year's activities. Examine and repair deficiencies from the previous year. Take care not to make it difficult for accounts receivable to follow up and collect. You are also burdened with poor debts. In terms of work and business, you will have internal and external disputes at the start of the year. Your task must be done with intention; otherwise, you risk losing your reputation. When signing an employment contract at this time, double-check it thoroughly. Keep an eye out for subordinates who are generating problems. Internal messages should be delivered clearly to avoid errors.

In terms of fortune, this wage is so low that it is bleeding money. Be wary of unanticipated emergency charges that can deplete the liquidity in your pocket. Gambling is thus illegal. Do not invest in unlawful enterprises since you may face serious criminal charges.

During this time, keep an eye out for criminals entering the house as well as other mishaps among family members. In terms of love, there are many conflicts over nonsense throughout this period. In terms of health, travelers must also be cautious about mishaps. Starting a new profession, engaging in joint ventures, and making other investments are all options for family and friends. This month is not going well.

Support Days: 3 Feb., 7 Feb., 11 Feb., 15 Feb., 19 Feb., 23 Feb., 27 Feb.
Lucky Days: 2 Feb., 14 Feb., 26 Feb
Misfortune Days: 5 Feb., 17 Feb., 29 Feb
Bad Days: 8 Feb., 20 Feb.

Month 2 in the Dragon Year (6 Mar 23 - 5 Apr 23)

The horoscope goes into an allied line this month. They also came upon the fortunate star "Tiang Tek" which was shining brightly. The mansion of Destiny shines like a rainbow. What you should do this month is conduct a survey to determine your readiness and bravery to take on large projects. Invest your money wisely and stick to your goals, since you will discover the power of support this month. Destiny is thus analogous to obtaining enough electricity to fully charge the battery. The journey of life has returned with renewed vigor. As a consequence, under calm and smooth conditions, money, work, and company are heading in the right route. Your rapid pursuit will lead you down the right path and ensure your future.

Patronage has been completely supported in the realm of employment, including business. When the tide comes in, it's an excellent moment to scoop up water. As a result, this is yet another month in which you should not sit idly by and allow a chance to pass you by. You should increase your efforts, produce results, and increase your sales and money for others to see. In terms of earnings, the figures are stunning. It all relies on your effort and how much you accomplish it and grow as a person.

In terms of money, the stars favor high liquidity this month. But it will be much better if the money is flowing freely. You must also join the fight alongside your coworkers. As a result, the outcomes will be obvious. The fortunes of the family are tranquil and get good energy. There will be wonderful news and joyous events in the house. This month is another excellent month for engagement, marriage, and good health in terms of easy love. However, be cautious of the possibility of injury and bleeding when working or traveling. In terms of eating, avoid excessive fat. Be cautious of pollutants that might cause blood disorders. Family and friends should avoid squabbles. You should avoid becoming involved in the disputes of your pals. This month is still a good time to start a new career, buy stocks, and make other investments.

Support Days: 2 Mar, 6 Mar., 10 Mar., 14 Mar., 18 Mar., 22 Mar., 26 Mar., 30 Mar
Lucky Days: 9 Mar, 21 Mar.
Misfortune Days: 12 Mar., 24 Mar.
Bad Days: 3 Mar., 15 Mar., 27 Mar

Month 3 in the Dragon Year (6 Apr 23 - 5 May 23)

Starting this month, when you go to a new month, the horoscope's path changes. Even in the previous month, the selected individual met several challenges. But it is a lesson, and you have the confidence to speak up correct what is wrong, and fill in the gaps. You have the opportunity to enter a new day of wonderful grandeur that awaits you. When the circumstances are good, it is not too late to begin battling.

This paycheck fortune's money is still coming in routinely; it's not extraordinary, and there's still not much luck, so it's not a smart idea to risk investing excessively; you'll lose more than you'll gain. Additionally, you should carefully organize your spending. Even if there are some challenges in business and commerce at this time, there is some fallout from the previous month. Please be calm and thoughtful when resolving issues. Consider previous errors to be lessons. Every difficulty can be solved satisfactorily. The essential thing to remember this month is that you must continue to enhance your diligence, work hard, develop yourself to identify possibilities, and expose yourself to new situations to compensate for the job delays of the previous month.

The family horoscope is serene. Even if there is no significant sickness, there is still nothing serious for you to be concerned about in terms of excellent love, beautiful relationships, and health. However, you must be alert and know how to control your drinking and eating. You should refrain from all forms of alcohol, including smoking and drinking less. Be stricter and more concerned about food safety. Because there will be more fire aspects this month. You are at risk of developing liver disease. You should cut back on foods like spicy meals, barbecuing, and excellent buddies. You will make pals who will assist you. This month has yet to provide a profit from stock trading and other investments.

Support Days: 3 Apr., 7 Apr., 11 Apr., 15 Apr., 19 Apr., 23 Apr., 27 Apr.
Lucky Days: 2 Apr., 14 Apr., 26 Apr.
Misfortune Days: 5 Apr., 17 Apr., 29 Apr.
Bad Days: 8 Apr., 20 Apr.

Month 4 in the Dragon Year (6 May 23 - 5 Jun 23)

The life path of persons born in the Year of the Snake will shift this month, even though their horoscope will improve. However, you cannot be negligent with health issues. Because illness will be discovered to impede employment. It also results in property loss. Take this opportunity to pay attention to your health, regulate your diet, keep proper eating and living cleanliness, and eat meals on time to avoid gastritis.

This month, you will also locate sponsors who will assist you with your job and help you advance. You may also have access to fresh prospects or relatives who might put you in the direction of long-term investing.

This wage wealth will be easy to come by. You will have the possibility to receive more money if you have other channels. However, you should also set aside funds for future rounds of investment. Don't be complacent about overspending. It will cause liquidity to contract, causing credit and negative reputation to deteriorate.

During this time in your family horoscope, you should pay more attention to the health of the elderly in your house and keep an eye on the home's security. In terms of love, it is not yet an impediment to the job ahead. Just don't set it off by telling old stories.

If you have poor health, you should be cautious about heart disease, high blood pressure, and stress. However, you should relax and let go. There will be nothing to obstruct your hearing or sight. Bullying is used to express feelings with others around you. This month's horoscopes of family and friends are still easy. Starting a new career, buying stocks, and making other investments are all options. Profits for some things will appear as attractive figures in the account.

Support Days: 1 May., 5 May., 9 May., 13 May., 17 May., 21 May., 25 May., and 29 May.

Lucky Days: 8 May., 20 May.
Misfortune Days: 11 May., 23 May.
Bad Days: 2 May., 14 May., 26 May.

Month 5 in the Dragon Year (6 Jun 23 - 6 Jul 23)

The fate requirements for persons born this month in the Year of the Snake have not yet passed the rainy season. Many storylines nevertheless necessitate keeping an eye on developments that may shift to the opposite side. Whether it's your profession or your business, you're at a crossroads this month, testing your talents and even confronting tougher competitors vying for market share. This month, avoid allowing your preconceptions to interfere with your work. While working, you must be cautious and have good emotional control. Use composure and tranquility, rather than those who talk improperly and erupt with emotion. You will most likely confront greater difficulties and entanglements as a result of this.

This income is adequate in terms of good fortune. You should also avoid anything excessive. Do not be avaricious. Gambling should be prohibited to avoid exacerbating the problem. However, buying stocks for investment has discovered a new route worth exploring. If you are prepared to acquire and hold shares.

Even at this stage, the family feels at peace. However, minors or subordinates causing disturbance must be avoided.

You will fight for your sweetheart in love, so consider carefully before doing anything.

In terms of health at this time, be wary of reoccurring illnesses and ailments, and avoid accidents at all costs.

In terms of employment, you should not begin a new project.

Support Days: 2 Jun., 6 Jun., 10 Jun., 14 Jun., 18 Jun., 22 Jun., 26 Jun., 30 Jun
Lucky Days: 1 Jun., 13 Jun., 25 Jun
Misfortune Days: 4 Jun., 16 Jun., 28 Jun
Bad Days: 7 Jun., 19 Jun.

Month 6 in the Dragon Year (7 Jul 23 - 7 Aug 23)

The horoscope of people born in the Year of the Snake enters the dangerous zone this month. You will encounter both good and unpleasant things. Even if you see a path, there is a fantastic opportunity ahead. However, you must be cautious of dark alleys that hide perils. During this period, both of you must be cautious of saying anything that is not worth listening to. It will put oneself at risk. You should accomplish some things this month, whether you're speaking or working. Don't let your lips outrun your emotions. Always consider before speaking and behave with caution. Work and company will face challenges and issues as a result of the monsoon wave. The most essential thing to remember this month is to be courteous, humble, and hardworking.

This month's financial situation is manageable. Direct income is still coming in as usual. The money from the windfall, however, must be taken at your own risk. As a result, you should avoid increasing your risk by spending money to test your luck in the stock lottery. Also, avoid anyone who loans you money and guarantees it. You should not invest in pirated or illegal firms, and you should also carefully control your income and spending. You should save some money in case of an emergency to avoid running out of funds.

The family horoscope is serene. This year, you are looking forward to welcoming important guests to your house.

There is still a method to strew rose petals, have a smooth connection, and have a companion and lover that cares and assists you properly.

You cannot be reckless with mishaps when traveling in terms of your health. If you consume alcohol, you should take public transit and be cautious of stomach and intestinal disorders.

Horoscopes of relatives during this time: Be wary of friends who betray you or want to deceive and take advantage of you.

You are likely to be duped if you start a new job, buy stocks, or make other investments this month. If you can avoid it, you should since it is better for your pocketbook.

Support Days: 4 Jul., 8 Jul., 12 Jul., 16 Jul., 20 Jul., 24 Jul., 28 Jul.
Lucky Days: 7 Jul., 19 Jul., 31 Jul.
Misfortune Days: 10 Jul., 22 Jul.

Bad Days: 1 Jul., 13 Jul., 25 Jul.

Month 7 in the Dragon Year (8 Aug 23 - 7 Sep 23)

With the arrival of this month, the Lord of Destiny's life path has turned upside down and downward. What was expected was discovered to be void. This month, you should evaluate your strengths. Work or commerce If you try to accomplish more than you can, you may end up causing more harm, and you should avoid interfering with other people's jobs since it will lead to difficulties later.

Problems will arise at work with coworkers, clients, or anyone with whom you must interact. As a result, you must be able to manage your emotions. Do not behave rashly or rashly. To minimize the power of a protracted dispute, you need also to learn to be modest.

Income will be reduced as a result of this wage increase. Financially, you will experience asset loss. You can employ a solution by purchasing items you want at the beginning of the month. This month, no loans will be granted. Reduce your entertainment, avoid gambling, avoid investing in illicit or pirated enterprises, and avoid thirst for money that is not yours.

The family's fortunes are bleak. Take precautions to avoid injury and blood loss from equipment, tools, or sharp items. Be wary of persons who embezzle, make errors, or fall victim to fraudsters.

For love is still hazy. You frequently argue. Take your time. Consider a time when you were still in love.
In terms of health, be wary of spinal cord injury and the danger of requiring surgery as a result of an accident.
People who bring relatives and friends to spend money are common. As a result, you should never lend money to anyone.
For beginning a new career, buying stocks, and making other investments Avoid being a victim of a cheater. Don't get taken in by gorgeous fantasy visuals and investing compliments.

Support Days: 1 Aug., 5 Aug., 9 Aug., 13 Aug., 17 Aug., 21 Aug., 25 Aug., 29 Aug.
Lucky Days: 12 Aug., 24 Aug.
Misfortune Days: 3 Aug., 15 Aug., 27 Aug
Bad Days: 6 Aug., 18 Aug., 30 Aug.

Month 8 in the Dragon Year (8 Sep 23 - 7 Oct 23)
This month, the fortunate star "Tiang Tek" will invigorate your destiny if you were born in the Year of the Snake. Many labor tasks will go effortlessly, requiring just half the effort, yet yielding returns that are more than 100%. As a result, this month, you should select a date of birth that will help you in your job activities, such as launching new items. Create or lead a project, create a new store, add a branch, or launch a new venture. You should work quickly to develop new work, enhance revenue, or increase productivity. At this point, the likelihood of success is great.

In terms of work, you will discover the strength of assistance from the favorable stars this month. However, you should prioritize developing positive relationships with people both inside and outside the organization. Everyone wants to connect with individuals who know how to be courteous and considerate.

This wage fortune may suffer a loss of assets. Both incomes are insufficient. There will be a cash outflow during the month. Please keep in mind that when it comes to money and gold, it will not be long before the money is returned.

The family horoscope is also supported by favorable energy. You have the requirements to arrange more auspicious events within the house, have an auspicious time to move into a new house or residence, launch a new store or branch, and add more members.

In terms of love, the love tree will bloom and yield fruit this month, and relationships will progress.

In terms of health, avoid air allergies and other allergens.

In terms of family and excellent friends, you will discover kind relatives who will assist you in resolving the situation.

To begin a new career, form a joint venture, or make other investments. Many things will see significant returns this month, making them worthwhile investments.

Support Days: 2 Sep., 6 Sep., 10 Sep., 14 Sep., 18 Sep., 22 Sep., 26 Sep., 30 Sep
Lucky Days: 5 Sep., 17 Sep., 29 Sep
Misfortune Days: 8 Sep., 20 Sep.
Bad Days: 11 Sep., 23 Sep..

Month 9 in the Dragon Year (8 Oct 23 - 6 Nov 23)

This month, the Year of the Snake's life path has not verticalized. You should be prepared and keep an eye out for any unforeseen developments. When it comes to work and business during this time, be aware that there will be challenges. Be wary of personal and external disputes that may grow into arguments. As a result, you must be extremely cautious with your own words and practice patience in all tasks. This month, you should do the following: Be aware and relaxed. Put a grin on your face when you meet someone. Please resolve any issues as soon as possible. Don't let things get out of hand.

This pay scale fluctuates. You should not invest in fortune money since it poses a huge risk. You must still manage your income and spend wisely. Reduce wasteful spending. This is also another month when you are not permitted to lend money to others or make financial commitments.

In terms of love, the relationship is still wonderful. Couples who are ready to marry might select an auspicious day this month to walk hand in hand and enter the wedding gate. In terms of health, be cautious of sickness, eye disease, high blood pressure, allergies, and the risks of fire and heat.

This month, be wary of dishonest persons in your family and circle of acquaintances. Be wary about being intimidated and deceived.

Starting a new job is not a smart idea. When it comes to stocks and other investments this month, you should start by looking at your budget.

Support Days: 4 Oct., 8 Oct., 12 Oct., 16 Oct., 20 Oct.
Lucky Days: 11 Oct., 23 Oct.
Misfortune Days: 2 Oct., 14 Oct., 26 Oct
Bad Days: 5 Oct., 17 Oct., 29 Oct.

Month 10 in the Dragon Year (7 Nov 23 - 6 Dec 23)

The person born in the Year of the Snake this month has reached the end of their life journey. Internal and external pressures will put a strain on business operations. This month, you should do the following: Do your job well. Do not interfere with the work of others. Visit both existing and new clients regularly to create and deepen connections.

There was a monsoon in terms of employment and trade. Be wary of internal disagreements that impede work development. And be aware that there will be disagreements with the individuals you must deal with. To reduce this, maintain positive interpersonal relationships with others around you and be modest. Respect for seniors can help you operate more efficiently.

In terms of finances, there were also unforeseen incidents this month that resulted in asset losses. Gambling is thus illegal. Do not engage in illicit activities, and most importantly, handle your funds carefully. You should also store some money as a backup in case of an emergency. Furthermore, don't be tricked into being selfish only for a minute; you might lose a lot of money. Be cautious when completing various contract paperwork during this period to avoid encountering fraudsters.

Horoscope for a medium-sized family. In terms of love, a third person will appear to intercede and seek to share your feelings. You must regulate yourself and handle situations with alertness and calm. It will cause additional disputes at home and worsen the fractures. In terms of health, keep an eye out for brain nerve illness. The condition produces cumulative stress to the point of inability to sleep and frequent dizziness. You must not drive if you have consumed alcohol.

Relatives and friends should be aware of falling into a trap because they may encounter persons with bad intentions who deceive, take advantage, and create sorrow. To begin a new employment, buy stocks, and make different investments. At this time, be wary of persons who are embezzlers or dishonest people searching for a quick buck.

Support Days: 1 Nov., 5 Nov., 9 Nov., 13 Nov., 17 Nov., 21 Nov., 25 Nov. , 29 Nov
Lucky Days: 4 Nov., 16 Nov. ., 28 Nov
Misfortune Days: 7 Nov., 19 Nov.
Bad Days: 10 Nov., 22 Nov.

Month 11 in the Dragon Year (7 Dec 23 - 5 Jan 24)

This month, the horoscopes of persons born in the Year of the Snake have once again entered the alliance's area. An auspicious star was also circling and glowing brightly. Today's path through life is as smooth and lovely as a brightly shining rainbow. You will flourish and advance in your career and business, and your requests will be granted again when the skies open their doors. What you should do this month is wait patiently and bravely for possibilities to present themselves. When you notice an open opportunity, decide fast to act and move forward. Good possibilities will pass you by if you only think about them and do nothing.

This time will see development in terms of labor and trade. You will be able to transform your effort into money and amass tremendous fortune. Some of you will be promoted or earn a wage raise. Please be diligent and develop work promptly to increase revenue. Because now is an excellent moment to invest, develop your business, produce more items, or introduce new ones.

This pay is generous. Money comes in from a variety of sources depending on what you have worked hard to invest in. The more careful you are, the faster your revenue will appear to expand tremendously.

There is a power of patronage to visit for the family horoscope. Another month with a smile on your face. Participated in applauding and celebrating the achievements of the people in the house, or else he had the qualifications to plan additional auspicious celebrations.

It's time to let the sunshine on love. Those who want to beg for love and beg for forgiveness. The odds of success are really good this month. It is also a suitable time for another month for any single folks who are eager to become engaged or enroll in a wedding ceremony.

It is stronger and better in terms of health. Family and friends are helpful. Starting a new job, investing in stocks, or other professions. This month is bright, with the color green.

Support Days: 3 Dec., 7 Dec., 11 Dec., 15 Dec., 19 Dec., 23 Dec., 27 Dec, 31 Dec.
Lucky Days: 10 Dec., 22 Dec.
Misfortune Days: 1 Dec., 13 Dec., 25 Dec.
Bad Days: 4 Dec., 16 Dec., 28 Dec.

Amulet for The Year of the Snake

"The Dragon Horse Sign was successful in every respect."

This year, those born in the Year of the Snake should set up and revere spiritual things. "The Dragon Horse Sign is prosperous in all ways" to improve your fortune. By putting it on a workstation or a cash register table. To make the intended person's business and trade run smoothly and profitably. Have a wealthy family and a serene and happy home.

It is claimed that people are part of the life on our planet. They are regulated by the rules of the cosmos, which are made up of cyclical symbols. This is connected to the 12 zodiac signs and numerous elements may be split into two qualities known as "10 branches of the sky and 12 branches of the earth" The effect of the universe's might will be reflected in the sky's ten branches. which correspond to the five elements and four directions on the compass disk, while the twelve earth stalks correspond to the twelve zodiac signs. During these 12 years of life, there will be both friends who promote and adversaries who destroy one another. All 12 years will focus on causing both merit and demerit. According to the year of birth and the reaction to the year of birth. Which relies on whether it would produce good or auspicious effects or create misery and disaster for the designated individual.

Those born in the year of the Snake or Mia Keng (destiny house) belong to the zodiac sign Ji. This year will bring both pleasant and negative experiences. Hard labor will yield results that are well worth the effort. However, you will have challenges to overcome along the road, or you will encounter coworkers who bully you. Other individuals find a way to have fun. Those who operate their enterprises will come across thorns that are tough to navigate. In love, you will meet someone you adore, but this is not the year to marry. Third parties should be avoided by individuals who are already married. In terms of health, keep on the lookout for intestinal issues this year, as well as mishaps when traveling. If you want to solve an issue, you should surround yourself with sacred things and wear auspicious pendants. "The Dragon Horse Sign is successful in all respects" to enhance work development, business prosperity, greater riches, and protection from calamities and many chaotic occurrences.

This Year of the Snake's auspicious things are: "The Horse-Dragon Sign is successful in all respects," which indicates your prosperity and good fortune. Inside the sign are two auspicious creatures, one of which is a "dragon," a symbol of strength and prestige who can turn evil things into good. Brings good fortune and riches. The "horse" is the second auspicious animal. It is a lucky sign that represents agility, agile commerce, and smooth, continuous cash flow. It is presented on a plaque with the fortunate pair of characters "Fugui" and "Ji Xiang," which indicate prosperity and infinite good fortune. As a result, it aids in making the fortunes of persons born in the Year of the Snake even more exceptional, delivering only complete and fortunate things. Work and finances are doing well, and fortune will rise during the year.

Those born in the Year of the Snake should also wear an auspicious pendant. "The Dragon Horse Sign is successful in every way." Wear it around your neck or carry it with you when traveling both near and far from home. So that you may be blessed with money and auspicious locations, as well as prosperity and advancement in business and commerce. All year, the family is tranquil and joyful. It generates greater and faster efficiency and effectiveness than previously.

Good Direction: Southeast, Southwest, and West
Bad Direction: Northwest
Lucky Colors: Red, Pink, Orange, and Green.
Lucky Times: 09.00 – 10.59, 15.00 – 16.59, 17.00 – 18.59.
Bad Times: 03.00 – 04.59, 21.00 – 22.59.

Good Luck For 2024

www.ingramcontent.com/pod-product-compliance
Lightning Source LLC
Chambersburg PA
CBHW051303160726
47994CB00003B/1288